1778-1780 TAX LISTS
OF
HENRY COUNTY, VIRGINIA

By Lela C. Adams

Southern Historical Press
Greenville, South Carolina

Copyright 1973
By: Lela C. Adams

Copyright Transferred 1983
To: Southern Historical Press, Inc.

All rights reserved. No part of this publication may be reproduced, stored in a retrieval system, transmitted in any form, posted on to the web in any form or by any means without the prior written permission of the publisher.

Please direct all correspondence and orders to:

www.southernhistoricalpress.com
or
**SOUTHERN HISTORICAL PRESS, Inc.
PO BOX 1267
Greenville, SC   29601**
southernhistoricalpress@gmail.com

ISBN #0-89308-361-5

Printed in the United States of America

At a meeting for the Commissioners for appointing assessors for the County of Henry at Abraham Penn's on Saturday, the 25th of April 1778.
Present: Edmund Lyne, Abraham Penn and William Tunstall.

John Cox is appointed Clerk of the said Commission.

Ordered that the different companies under the several Captains of the Militia of the County be the several districts for the Assessors of the said County.

John Pyrtle and Humphrey Scraggins are appointed to assess the respective persons property in the district of the Company of Militia under the said Command of the said Pyrtle and return an account of their proceedings according to law.

John Blagge and Richard Tankersley the same

Frederick Reeves and William Graves, Sr., the same

William Cook and Thomas Jones the same

Jessee Clay and James Cowden the same

John Alexander, Jr. and Andrew Ray the same

David Lenear and Alexander McKain the same

Thomas Cooper and James Anthony the same

Mordicia Hord and John Barksdale the same

Thomas Henderson and Isaac McDonald the same

James Shelton and James Spencer the same

Stephen Heard and William Swanson, Jr. the same

Jonathan Hanby and William Smith the same

James Lyon and Eliphaz Shelton the same

Robert Stockton and Daniel Smith the same

James Poteet and Blackmore Hughes the same

Robert Woods and Robert Mason the same

Hugh Armstrong and Abraham Byrd the same

Thomas Stockton and John Parr the same

Whereas the said assessors received their instructions and are as followeth: We, the Commissioners of Henry County being visited by law with sufficient authority for this purpose have appointed you assessors to assess the respective persons property as aforesaid. And that you may be enabled to act with propriety we have transcribed such parts of the Act as are necessary for your directions, and have added such instructions for your proceedings as are proper for your complying with the true intention of the Act. The law says that a tax or rate of Ten Shillings for every hundred pounds value shall be paid for all Mannors, Messuages, Land and Tenenants, slaves, mulattos, servants to thirty-one years of age. Horses, mules and silver plate, on the first day of August 1778. That the like rate of ten shillings for every hundred pounds shall be paid for all money exceeding five pounds in the possession of one person by the possessor therefore on the said 1st day of August. That a tax of two shillings for every pound be paid for the amount of the annual interest received upon all debts bearing interest. Also the amount of all annuities. That a tax of ten shillings a wheel upon all riding carriages, four pence per herd of all neat cattle and five shillings per poll upon all tithables above the age of twenty-one years, except soldiers, sailors, parish poor and such as receive an annual allowance in consideration of wounds or injuries received in the Public Service except also slaves, mulatto servants to thirty-one years of age who being property are rated at their value as aforesaid shall be paid by the owner or person enlisting such carriages and tithables respectively on the said 1st day of August. That a tax of ten shillings for every hundred pounds of the amount of all salaries, and of the neat income of all offices or profit those of the military and sea officers in the Service of the United States of America or other of them in respect of their employmnents only excepted on the said 1st day of August. That a tax of six pence per gallon for all spiritious liquors hereafter distilled in this Commonwealth to be paid by the distiller or distilled in any of the United States of America and imported into this land or by water at any time before the 1st day of December 1784. And that every person who hath not taken the Oath or Affirmation of Allegiance to this State required to be taken by an Act of the last session of Assembly and shall not take the same before the 1st day of May next and who shall fail to produce to you a Certificate of his having taken such Oath or Affirmation shall pay double the several rate and taxes aforesaid for such property and tithables hereby subject to taxation as he shall be owner of or shall be in his family. Within five days after receiving notice of your appointment and before you enter upon your business you are to go together before one of us or before a Justice of the Peace and take the following oath or being a Quaker or a Menoist shall affirm or declare to the same effect. To wit: J.A.B. do swear I will truly execute the duty of an assessor and faithfully justly and impartially assess the pound rate imposed by the Act of Assembly for that purpose upon all property within my hundred liable thereto according to the best of my skill and judgment and the directions of the said Act. And therein will spare none for favor or affection nor any person aggrevive for hatred, malice or ill will. So help me God. After you have taken the Oath or Affirmation you are personally to apply to every person within your district or hundred and require them respectively to give an account on oath which either of you may administer of all lands, slaves, mulatto, servants to thirty-one years of age. Horses, mules, silver plate and interest received which shall become due after passing the Act on debts bearing interest, all annuities except a public provision for wounded soldiers and their families, all riding carriages, neat cattle and tithable persons above the age of twenty-one years, not being soldiers, sailors, or parish poor or persons receiving allowances for wounds received in the Public Service, slaves or servants to thirty-one years of age which each such person is the owner or belong to or reside in his or her family or which he or she is in possession of as guardian to any orphan or are Executor or Administrator of the Estate of Any person deceased. And also an account or near as can be judged of all spirituous liquors distilled or imported by land or by water by any such person from or after passing the Act. And every person is also

to make Oath that he or she hath not shifted or changed the
possession of any this said taxable articles or use any fraud,
covin or device in order to evade the assessment thereof. You
are to require all persons in your district having public salaries to render an account of the amount thereof. You are also
to call persons holding offices of profit, except military or
sea officers, in respect of their employments and residing in
your district to render and account upon Oath to the best of
their knowledge of the neat annual income of such office. All
and every species of which property so give in or which you
shall by other wages or means discover destinelly inter against
the name of the owner or person charged with the tax thereon and
proceed to value the lands, slaves, horses, mules and plate so
given in and discovered as the same would in your judgment sell
for in ready money having regard to the local situation of land
and other circumstances and in case you should differ on opinion
in the price or value of anything you are in that case to split
the difference and set down the middle rate as its value. You
are to extend the value against each species of property and set
down in a distinct column the amount of the pound rate or tax
hereby imposed upon the whole of such property belonging to each
person as well as of the taxes of another nature imposed hereby
upon such person. And you are to give such person a memorandum
in writing of such pound rate or tax to enable him or her to pro-
vide for payment thereof in due time and where a tract of land
belonging to any person residing or having a plantation with
slaves thereon shall lie in two or more hundreds the same shall
be valued by the assessors of that hundred werein the proprietor
lives or hath a plantation and if the owner doth not reside or
there be no plantation thereon, then the lands shall be assessed
in that hundred wherein the greatest quantity thereof shall lie,
and in such case the assessors shall enter the County in which
the proprietor lives if they are informed thereof. When you
shall have thus valued all the said taxable property in your
district you are to make a fair return of all your proceedings
to us. Entering the names of the persons assessed in alphitical
order with the species and value of their property and the pound
rate thereon as aforesaid and you are therein to enter you own
names with each distinct species of taxable property you sever-
ally own or possess which we shall value after examining you on
Oath. All silver plate in your district is to be valued at ten
shillings per ounce weight and no more. A Clause in the Act
inacts that all lands under lease for an annual rent and subject
to the tax shall be valued without regard to such rent but where
such valuations shall exceed twenty years purchase computed upon
the annual rent to be ascertained by the assessors they shall
proceed to assess the landlords the pound rate upon the amount
of twenty years purchase of the rent, and shall assess the pound
rate upon the residue of the value of the land and distinguish
such proportions in their return and where such rent shall be
received in tobacco or other commodity the assessor shall value
the same in money in order to adjust such proportions between
landlords and tenants. Where any tenant at an annual rent shall
be willing to pay the pound rate assessed on his landlord for
the land held by such tenant it shall be lawful for him or her
to do so and the collectors receipt for the same shall entitle
him or her to a deduction for the amount thereof out of the rent
and where the landlord shall reside out of this Commonwealth or
have no visiable estate thereon to levy the pound rate for the
value of his land in such case the said pound rate shall be paid
by or levied upon the tenant or tenants on said land not exceeding the annual amounts of the rents and allowed to him or her
aforesaid. You are to make a return of all your proceedings to

us, the Commissioners, in not less than four weeks nor more than six weeks from the time you receive your orders and instructions. You are liable to a penalty of Fifty Pounds each in case you should refuse to act and do the duty for assessor unless you or either of you have a sufficient excuse to be judge by us, the Commissioners.
And then they adjourned till the 25th day of June.

         Edmund Lyne
         Will. Tunstall
         Abram. Penn

At a meeting of the Commissioners at Henry Courthouse on Thursday the 25th day of June 1778, present, Edmund Lyne, Abraham Penn and William Tunstall, Commissioners. Robert Stockton and Daniel Smith, two of the assessors returned an account of their proceedings agreeable to Law and the same was ordered to be recorded.

James Shelton and James Spencer the same

Thomas Stockton and John Parr, same

Robert Wood and Robert Mason, same

Blackmore Hughes and James Poteet, same

John Pyrtle and Humphrey Scoggins, same

William Cook and Thomas Jones, same

Stephen Heard and William Swanson Jr., same

Thomas Cooper and James Anthony, same

John Fleming and John Wells, same

Thomas Henderson and Isaac McDonald, same

John Blagge and Richard Tankersley, same

James Cowden and Jessee Clay, same

Frederick Reeves and William Graves, same

Nothing more being offered the Commissioners adjourned until Tuesday the 14th July next.

At a Meeting of the Commissioners at Henry Courthouse on Tuesday the 14th day of July 1778, present: Edmund Lyne, Abraham Penn and William Tunstall.

Jonathan Hanby and William Smith returned their account
Hugh Armstrong and Abraham Byrd, the same
Mordicai Hord and John Barksdale, the same

And the proceeding of the assessors aforesaid as follows, to wit:

Alexander, John, Sr.; John, Jr. William	Allen, Micajah
Anderson, Armistead	Adams, Jacob; William
Allen, John	Atkins, David
Armstrong, Hugh	Atkinson, Joel
	Adams, Richard

Acton, James
Anthony, James
Allen, Samuel
Arnold, Henry
Allen, George
Arnold, William
Akins, Nichols
Acuff, John
Alsop, James
Allsop, Thomas, Sr.; Thomas, Jr.; John
Arthur, John
Archer, William
Anthony, Joseph
Alexander, William; John
Anderson, James
Anglin, Phillip; Mary; Joseph
Atkinson, Jessee
Auksman, Nicholas - Dbl. Taxed
Anderson, James
Alley, Nickolas
Armstrong, Francis
Atkins, Jacob
Anderson, John

Bush, Thomas
Blevins, John, Jr.
Bailey, Thomas
Blevins, William, Sr.
Bouldin, Joseph
Blevins, Dillion; William, Jr.
Bolling, James
Bunch, David
Bolling, John, Jr.; John, Sr.
Bowman, Robert; William
Byrd, Abraham; Abraham, Jr.
Bayler, Peter
Bartlett, John
Biggs, Henry
Bartlett, Nathan - Dbl. Taxed
Bullock, John - Dbl. Taxed
Boyler, John - Dbl. Taxed
Bartletts Heirs
Barker, Joseph
Bakrer, John
Bailey, Carr
Barker, John - Dbl. Taxed; Charles
Bradberry, Henry
Barksdale, John; Henry
Bell, William
Buzzard, Phillip - Dbl. Taxed
Barritt's Heirs
Bradley, Laurance
Bowman, John
Belcher, Thomas
Baker, Robert
Butterworth Orphans-Bedford Co.
Birks, John
Blevins, Willoughby
Bouding, William
Barker, Michael
Bartlett, William

Bernard, Charles
Bramer, James; Burgess
Bryant, Josiah
Brock, John
Baker, Edward
Butler, John
Blair, Joseph
Birks, Rowland
Bays, Peter, Sr. - Dbl. Taxed Peter, Jr. - Dbl. Taxed
Baker, Richard
Birks, William
Barrott, John
Bartton, William
Burdge, Woody
Brown, Augustine
Bolling, Christopher, Jr.
Burnett, Charles
Bradberry, Joseph
Bolling, Christopher, Sr.
Byrd, Samuel
Bolling, Anthony
Baughan, Henry; Avis (Arvis); Reuben
Briscoe, John
Bolling, William; James
Boatman, Richard
Brown, William
Brock, Joshua
Bates, Joseph
Bolling, Joseph
Bocock, John
Bolling, Archibald
Burns, John; Andrew
Bell, John
Beck, Paul
Barton, Joshua
Biba, John
Brillaman, Jacob-Dbl. Tax; Jacob, Sr.-Dbl. Tax
Bates, John
Bohanan, John
Bell, William
Bates, Sarah
Ballard, Richard
Belcher, Isham
Barnett, Nathan
Bolton, Robert; Thomas
Blashingham, Phillip
Bolling, Samuel
Burshire, Phillip, Sr.
Burshears, Phillip, Jr.
Bridges, Thomas
Bolling, John
Burton, William
Blankinship, John
Brogan, Phillip-Dbl. Tax
Bohanan, William
Barns, Adam
Barton, David
Briant, John-Dbl. Tax
Bohanan, Joshua
Bolling, William-Dbl. Tax

Blanket, Peter
Bernard, William
Blagg, John
Birch, Jarrard; John, Sr.;
  John, Jr.

Cox, John, Clerk; Taliaferro
Chowning, John
Cantwell, Adam
Cheek, Jesse
Cox, John - Mayo
Cloud, Joseph, Sr.
Cox, Jacob; Phillip
Cheek, Richard-Db. Tax
Cox, Samuel
Carlan, Daniel, Capt.
Carroll, Cornelius
Cheek, Richard
Cox, Benjamin
Cannon, Samuel
Cox, David - Montgomery
Cook, Jesster - Dbl. Tax
Collier, Richard
Chadwell, David
Collier, John; Charles
Cox, William, Jr.
Carter, Baines; Josiah;
  James
Camron, John
Critz, Hamon, Jr.; Hamon, Sr.
Collier, Richard - Dbl. Tax
Camron, Joseph
Cogar, Jacob (Koger); Henry
Cannon, Benjamin
Casey, Daniel
Crowley, Elizabeth
Chiles, Henry
Claunch, Jeremiah - Montgomery
Claunet, Jeremiah, Jr.
Cogar, John (Koger); Nicholas-
  Dbl. Tax
Cannaday, William
Chisum, Elijah
Carter, George
Cooper, Thomas, Jr.; Joseph;
  John; Thomas, Sr.
Copland, Peter; Richard
Crouch, John
Cunningham, John
Casleel, Abednigo
Cave, Robert
Coulls, Patrick, Adm.
Clowen, Michael
Crouch, John, Sr.
Combs, John
Conway, James
Callaway & Early
Cummins, Thomas
Carter, Joseph
Cooley, James
Callaway, James, Col.
Chandler, Joseph
Collier, John

Carter, David
Cook, William; James
Cloud, William
Cockram, Edward-Dbl. Tax;
  Sarah
Cox, Charles
Cobler, Thomas - Dbl. Tax
Cox, Russell - Dbl. Tax
Cole, Stephen
Carter, Bailey
Cowden, William
Cockerham, William
Cowden, James
Clackson, David
Cowan, Robert - Dbl. Tax
Craget, Peter
Cockerham, Abner
Choice, William; Tully,
  Sr.; Tully, Jr.
Crist, Elizabeth
Chandler, Benjamin
Clack, Spencer
Carter, Josiah for Carter's
Casterson, William
Cantwell, John
Carrill, Judith
Clay, Jessee
Collier, John, Leatherwood
Cox, James; Francis

Dunn, Michael
Davis, John
Dunn, Waters, Sr.; Waters,
  Jr.
Davidson, William
Dodson, Charles
Duncan, George
Dillion, Henry; Benjamin
Dickenson, James; John
Dickins, Richard
Dodson, Lambath
Dillard, John
Durham, Gregory
Depriest, Randolph; Tabitha
Denny, James
Davis, Cornelius
Duncan, John-Dbl. Tax
Dickins, William
Duncan, John; Catharine
Daniel, John, Jr.
Denson, William
Donald, Robert-Chesterfield
Dunn, Richard
Dillingham, John; Michael
Dunlap, Henry
Dickson, John
Davis, Solomon
Dodd, John-Dbl. Tax
Duvall, Skinner Benjamin
Davis, Lewis; Jacob
Dillingham, Joshua; William,
  Sr.; William, Jr.
Davis, William

Douton, John
Davis, Johnathan
Dicks, James
Dobbs, John
Dogett, Miller
Dunn, William
Dodd, William; John
Dewiess, Lewis
Dillindine, Jacob-Dbl. Tax
Dorma, James
Daniel, George
Davis, John
Dillion, James
Daniel, John, Sr.; Reuben
Duncan, Martin
Donelson, Isaac
Doyal, John
Dickerson, Thompson

Estes, Elisha, Jr; Elisha-
  minor
Ellis, John
Estes, Bottom; Elisha, Sr.
Edward, Abel
Estes, Joel
East, William; John
Evans, Andrew
East, James
Elkins, James; Nathaniel
Epperson, Joseph
Evans, William; Major
Estes, William
Elkins, James; Ralph, Jr.;
  Ralph (Shoemaker); Jessee;
  Ralph, Sr.
Earley, Joseph
Eubanks, William
Evans, William
Elliott, George
Ellis, Joseph
Edwards, James, Jr.; Isham;
  William; Thomas, Jr.;
  William, Jr.; Thomas, Sr.;
  James, Sr.
Eakin, James
Elkins, William

Finch, Charles; John
Farris, William
Finch, Thomas
Faulkner, William-Dbl. Tax
Forbes, Charles
Frazier, Abraham
France, Mary; Peter
Fee, Thomas, Jr.; Thomas, Sr.
  (Both Dbl. Tax)
France, Henry
Fee, William-Dbl. Tax
Fulkerson, Frederick
Farrell, John
Foley, Bartholomew; Luke-Dbl.
  Tax
Flowers, Thomas

Fletcher, John
Flood, Comfort
Fortune, Joseph
Fleming, John
Farguson, John, Sr.; John,
  Jr.-Dbl. Tax
Frazer, Robert
Farguson, Joseph
Fitzgerald, Frederick
Felps, Solomon
Farguson, William
Fewson, John
Felphs, Mary

Greer, Acquilla; William
Goff, John
Gilliam, Peter
Grimmet, John
Gravly, Bittersworth
Gordon, Archibald
Graves, William
Glassres, John
Garrot, Joseph
Going, John
Gussett, John
Godward, James
Gresham, John
Gooch, Rachel
Gibson, Thomas; Andrew
Golden, Jacob
Gardner, William - Smith R.
Gibson, Randolph
Goff, Thomas
Grymer, Francis
Gibson, John
Green, James
Going, David
Green, John
Gates, James
Gillingtine, John
Goode, John
Gardner, Thomas; William,
  Capt.
Garner, Thomas
Grimmit, Robert
Grayham, Archibald
Gray, Samuel
George, William; John
Golsby, Daniel
Gates, Phillip; Samuel
Greer, Thomas; Moses, Sr.-
  Dbl. Tax; Uriah; William-
  Dbl. Tax; Shadrack-Dbl.
  Tax
Gwilliams, Edgecomb
Grimmit, Robert
Gilley, Francis-Dbl. Tax;
  Francis, Jr.; Charles, Jr.
Grogan, John
Gilliam, Debrix
Grogan, Thomas-Dbl. Tax
Goodwin, Joseph
Graves, William, Jr.

Grimmit, John
Gravely, Joseph

Haynes, Henry, Sr.; Henry, Jr.
Hale, Lewis
Heard, Jessee; William
Haynes, George
Heard, John; George; Thomas
Haynes, William
Hammon, William; Benjamin
Hodges, Joseph
Hall, William
Harden, Elepus (Elexus)
Hall, Lance
Hubbard, Eusebus
Hutchinson, Phillip
Haskins, William
Hodges, Isham; William
Hill, Isham
Huckaby, John
Hodges, William
Huckaby, Robert
Hall, Jessee
Hembrick, Nimrod
Hall; John; Mary
Holt, Richard
Hall, John - The Hollow
Harrington, John; James (both Dbl. Tax)
Holt, Phillip - Dbl. Tax
Holder, John - Dbl. Tax
Hill, Thomas - Dbl. Tax
Hollinsworth, Derrick - Dbl. Tax
Hanby, Jonathan
Hensley, Benjamin, Capt.; Benjamin Jr.-Dbl. Tax
Hamilton, Francis
Hensley, James
Hudson, Obediah
Howell, Paul
Hamilton, Thomas
Hickumbottom, William
Hensely, Benjamin, Sr.-Dbl. Tax
Hensley, Henry-Dbl. Tax; Hickman-Dbl. Tax
Hollandsworth, Thomas; William
Haley, David
Hunter, William
Hord, Mordicai
Hughes, Archs., Col.
Hawkins, Benjamin
Hencher, Obediah
Hamilton, Thomas
Hurt, Joseph
Hairston, Robert
Hall, Nathan; Sarah
Hubbard, Thomas
Harrill, William
Hughes, Blackmore
Hubbard, Benjamin
Harbour, Joel; Esais-Dbl. Tax
Hoff, Samuel; Thomas
Harris, Peter

Henderson, John
Hilton, Paul
Holder, John
Hutchinson, Richard
Halbert, William
Hudson, Peter
Hinton, William
Hilton, Samuel
Harris, Moses-Dbl. Tax; Henry
Heard, William, Sr.; William, Jr.
Hubbard, Harrison
Heard, John
Hairston, George
Hamilton, George
Hairston, Peter
Hill, Swinfield; Thomas
Holt, Ambrose
Hill, Violett
Hodges, Robert
Hagard, James-Dbl. Tax
Holloway, John
Houser, Jasper
Holcomb, Grymes
Hensley, Benjamin
Holladay, Robert
Hager, John
Hayse, William
Harbour, Elisha
Hunter, Alexander
Harris, Robert
Hamilton, Thomas, Esquire
Hardman, William; John
Harbour, Joyce
Harmer, John - Great Britian
Hick's Executors
Hammon, Joseph
Haile, Thomas
Hough, Joseph; Samuel-Dbl. Tax
Haile, Joseph, Sr.-Dbl. Tax; Joseph, Jr.-Dbl. Tax
Hunt, James
Hill, Thomas
Hancock, Thomas
Hooker, Mary
Hopper, Thomas
Hooker, Robert, Sr.; John; Robert, Jr.
Harmer & King-Great Britian
Heard, Stephen
Humpheys, Morris
Hicks, James-Brunswick
Handy, John

Innes, Hugh, Capt.
Ivie, Elisha; Lott
Ingram, John; James
Ison, John; William; Charles; Jonathan; James
Ivie, Howell

Jenkins, Lewis
Jamison, John; William
Jones, Ambrose
Jamison, Thomas
Jones, Thomas-Dbl. Tax
Jourdon, Hezekiah; Thomas; Jacob-Dbl. Tax
Jones, William, Sr.
James, John
Jourdon, Samuel
Jennings, Miles
Jones, John, Sr.; George
Jamison, John
Johnson, William
James, Jamey
Jarvis, Alexander
Johnson, James; Hudson
Jonakan, John
Jamison, Thomas-Marrowbone
Joyce, Alexander
Jones, Robert, Jr.; Henry; John, Robert, Sr.; Thomas, Jr.; Abraham; Isaac; Thomas, Sr.
Johnson, Samuel

Kerby, Joseph; Jessee
Kemp, John
Kerby, Francis; John
Keen, William; Carrill; John; Elisha
Kerby, David; Jessee
King, Walter-Great Britian
Keith, Cornelius-Dbl. Tax
King, Joseph
Kindrick, John
Kerby, Richard
Kelly, Barnabas
King, John
Kelly, Andrew; William; William, Jr.
Keel, James
Kiel, John
Kelly, John
Kindrick, Preston-Dbl. Tax
Kington, Francis

Law, John, Sr.; William; John, Jr.; Nathaniel
Lewis, Joseph
Long, William
Lunsdell, John; Jeremiah; John, Jr.
Loving, Mary
Lyne, Edmund; Henry
Long, John
Launders, Benjamin-Dbl. Tax
Linsey, Sarah
Login, Samuel
Lowe, Zadock; John; Samuel
Lankford, Robert
Lynch, William
Lawson, James

Lyon, James
Lawson, William; Moreman; John
Lomax, Randolph, Harmer & Co.
Lanier, Samuel; David
Lee, Stephen
Long, Christopher
Levesey, Thomas
Lyall, Alexander
Laws, Thomas
Lawson, David
Leath, Thomas
Lovell, William
Lamb, Walter
Loyd, James

Mead, William-Bedford
McKain, Alexander
Moore, Benjamin
Mays, David
Major, John
Mays, Sherwood; Henry; Abraham
Mosley, Thomas
Meirs, Stephen
McKain, Hugh
Magers, James
Milam, Samuel
Maxey, Walter
Meredith, James; William
Martin, Brice
Moore, Rhodham
Martin, Joseph
McPeak, Ezekiel
McGown, John, Sr.-Dbl. Tax; David-Dbl. Tax; Samuel Dbl. Tax
Mathews, John
Morris, Joseph; Samuel
May, James; Ambrose
Mattenlee, Walter
McCraw, William; Jacob
McKinney, Kinney
Manning, John
Matlock, David
Meredith, Bradley-Dbl. Tax; Junor
Minter, John
Musick, Elepus-Dbl. Tax
McKeary, John
Mayo, Valentine
Morran, Thomas
Morrison, Thomas
McAlexander, William
Murrell, Thomas
McAdoe, Ann
McDonald, Isaac
Miller, John
Marr, John
Murris, Thomas
Mankin, James
Morris, George-Dbl. Tax

Midkiff, Thomas
McBride, Patrick
McConway, Caleb; John
Mitchell, Robert; John-Dbl. Tax
Murrell, Jeffery; Richard
Mabry, George
McBride, Daniel
Murphy, William
Moore, John
Moseley, Mordicai
Manifee, William, Sr.; William, Jr.
Miller, George
Martin, James; Hugh
Mustin, Jean
McGeehee, Holden
Maddox, Michael
Martin, John, Capt-Woods to pay
Mason, Robert
McCoy, Richard
Miller, Thomas; Joseph
Murphy, John
Mead, Robert
Mavity, William; Robert
Mullings, Richard-Dbl. Tax; William, Jr.; William, Sr.; Ambrose; John
Morgan, John
May, Caleb
Maxey, Samson
Malin, John-Dbl. Tax
Mannin, Elizabeth; Davis
Manifee, John
Moore, William-Guilford
Mills, William-Hanover
Medcalf, Joseph
McLaughlin, John
Morton, James
Manley, Joseph
Milton, James
Miller, John
Morton, John(2)

Nowling, John; Richard
Newman, Joseph
Nelson, Thomas
Nicholls, John
Newman, John; Daniel
Neavell, John
Nance, Reubeen
Northcut, John
Noe, Pryor; John; John, Jr.
Nunn, Thomas
Norrick, Jacob-Dbl. Tax
Newton, Richard
Nash, Marvell

Oakley, Thomas; Richard; James
Oliver, James
Oneal, Susanna
O'Briant, Dennis-Dbl. Tax
Oldham, John; Thomas

Potter, Benjamin; Lewis
Powell, Robert
Prunty, James
Parberry, James
Prewitt, David, Jr.; David, Sr.
Potter, Thomas
Patterson, Samuel
Prunty, Thomas
Perryman, Richard
Powell, Robert-for Mary Hubbard
Paxton, Joseph-Dbl. Tax
Price, Joseph-Pwhatan
Pendleton, Benjamin
Pool, Micajah; George
Payne, John; Thomas
Pace, John
Payne, Reubun
Patterson, Jarrett
Polley, John
Pilgrim, Amos
Prater, Nehamiah
Poleston, Andrew-Mayo
Penn, Abraham
Parlsey, Richard
Parsley, Abraham; John; Thomas
Poteet, James
Poleson, Andrew
Prater, Archibald
Peregay, Edward
Prater, Jonathan
Pulliam, John
Parker, Samuel
Pace, George, Sr.; George, Jr.
Pilgrim, Amos
Poore, William
Pilgrim, William
Proze, Conrad-Dbl. Tax
Pigg, James
Pettigoe, Robert
Pearson, Robert
Picklemer, John-Dbl. Tax
Peirson, Joseph
Pyrtle, John
Parrott, Thorp
Packwood, Samuel; Richard
Perryman, Robert
Posey, Humphry
Pelphry, John
Polley, Edward
Prewit, Richard; Charles
Parr, John, Jr.
Posey, Francis
Parker, John
Peck, Jonathan; George
Peek, James
Prater, Ninion
Parr, John, Sr.
Perryman, Ro., exec. of John Perryman

Picard, John
Perkins, Nicholas Levins
Phillips, George
Pickles, David

Redmond, James
Rucker, Gideon
Richardson, Amos; Amos, Jr.
Ryan, William
Randolph, Samuel
Raly, Shelton
Roberson, Thomas; Thomas, Jr; John, Richard
Rae, Thomas-Dbl. Tax
Rowland, George
Richardson, Daniel
Ridle, Moses
Rae, James, Sr.
Roberson, William-Pr. George
Ramey, Daniel
Ryon, Phillip
Redd, John
Riger, Jacob
Rice, William
Rea, James, Jr.
Ramey, John
Ray, Andrew
Roberts, Joseph; James
Redman, Rodham
Reynolds, Bartlett; Nathaniel,Sr.
Richards, Thomas
Reynolds, William
Radliff, John
Reynolds, Richard
Russell, John
Reynolds, John
Randolph, Manns Thomas of Goochland
Rice, Spencer; Daniel
Rentfro, Jessee
Reynolds, Susanah; Richard (Leatherwood); Spencer
Ray, John
Rentfro, John
Ryan, Darby
Rentfro, James
Rawson, Charles
Reubell, Owen
Roberts, Thomas
Ross, Daniel
Radford, John-Dbl. Tax
Reel, Michael
Roach, John
Rice, Benjamin
Rea, John-Blacksmith
Ritch, William
Reno, John; Stephen
Rea, William-Dbl. Tax
Rickman, John
Reeves, George
Rowland, Baldwin; John, Sr.; Michael; John, Jr.
Rogers, David; George

Reynods, Richard - Smith R.
Royall, John
Richards, Edward
Ramsey, John; George-Dbl. Tax
Roads, Christian
Ramsey, Thomas
Richardson, Stannup
Rentfro, Joshua
Rickman, William
Rentfro, William
Rice, John-Pittsylvania

Smith, Guy
Senter, Stephen
Swanson, William, Sr.; Nathan; John
Shrewsberry, Jeremiah
Smith, John
Standefore, Israel
Smith, John
Standefore, Israel
South, Joseph
Sullivan, John
Smith, Thomas
Shockley, Levie
Smith, John
Street, Anthony-Lunenburgh
Swanson, William, Jr.
Stokes, John; George
Salmon, John
Sims, Ignatious
Simmons, John
Scruggs, Julius
Salmon, Hezekiah
Stewart, John
Sharp, John; Richard
Staunton, John
Stevens, John; Salomon
Sanders, John
Stuart, John-Dbl. Tax
Stewart, James-Dbl. Tax
Smith, John; Zachariah-Guilford
Sullivan, John
Sams, James
Smith, Bradley; Anthony
Shelton, Ralph
Smith, Josiah
Sowell, Joseph
Sturgeon, William
Soloman, Drury
Shelton, James
Spencer, James
Smith, Bartlett
Solomon, Isham
Smith, Munford
Stevens, William
Smith, William; John; Randolph
Serjant, -----
Sample, Deborah
Smith, Elizabeth

Short, James-Dbl. Tax
Smith, William; Isaac
Stockton, Agness
Smith, Solomon; Thomas
Short, Henry
Smith, Samuel
Ship, Joseph
Stockton, Thomas
Smith, Zadock-Dbl. Tax
Shelton, John
Stewart, William
Sandford, George; John
Seasay, James
Sharp, William
Sprangler, Daniel-Dbl. Tax
Shepard, Thomas
Staunton, Thomas
Stout, Joseph-Dbl. Tax
Sheridan, Phillip
Smith, Daniel
Senter, John-Dbl. Tax
Stanley, John
Saunders, Peter
Stanley, Richard
Stockton, Robert
Stout, Samuel
Stanley, William, Jr.; William Sr.; Robert
Sams, William
Street, Samuel
Stevens, William
Stevins, John
Scogins, George
Scales, Joseph-Dbl. Tax
Stallings, Jacob
Sprathey, James

Sneed, John
Scogan, Humphy
Sunter, Henry; George
Seearcy, Robert
Stamps, John
Smith, Daniel
Shelton, Ralph, Sr.
Simms, Sarah
Shelton, Eliphaz
Sims, Bartlett
Smith, Henry
Sism, Mathew
Shelton, James; Ezekiah; Jeremiah; Azariah
Small, John; Mathew
Stinnett, Benjamin
Salmon, Rowland
Slater, Joseph
Shores, Richard
Seamons, Joseph; Zachariah
Shoat, Isham-Dbl. Tax
Sinat, Richard
Stewart, James, Sr.; James Jr.; David
Shoat, Edward, Sr.; Edward, Jr.-Dbl. Tax; Austin
Stober, Jacob
Standifore, James, Sr.; James, Jr.; William; Luke
Shoat, Sebert
Swann, Jonathan
Sams, Edmuns; William, Sr.

List ends here - back sheets appear to be lost.

An alphabetical list of the taxes or pound rate imposed on the different persons property in the County of Henry and delivered to John Salmon, Sherif of the said County to collect for the year 1779.

Alley, Nicholas
Aukerman, Nicholas-Treble Tax; Daniel
Archer, William
Adkins, Jacob; David
Anderson, James; Peter; Jonas
Adkerson, Joel
Akin, James
Anthony, James
Adams, Thomas; Abraham; Jacob; William
Allen, Samuel
Akin, Nicholas
Acuff, John
Arthur, John
Anthony, Joseph
Anglin, Phillip; Joseph
Anderson, Armistead

Allen, Fisher
Alexander, John, Jr.; William
Abington, John
Acton, James
Armstrong, James
Allen, George
Armstrong, Hugh - 200 acres in Pittsylvania Co.
Allen, John

Barton, Isaac; David
Beakler, David
Bybe, John
Beek, Paul
Bates, John
Bohanan, Joshua
Bell, William

Bybe, Sherwood
Bartee, William
Barton, Susannah
Bates, John, Jr.
Blackeley, Robert
Beaver, Robert
Boyd, Robert
Barns, Adam
Boles, George
Bohanan, John
Bolling, Joseph
Bryant, Dennis; John
Brogan, Phillip
Boulton, Robert
Ballard, Richard
Burdit, Garvis-for Cowan
Bouton, Thomas
Blassingham, Phillip
Bolling, Samuel; Samuel for Guy Smith
Beaver, James
Brock, Joshua
Burton, Seth
Blankenship, Isham, Sr.; Isham, Jr.
Belcher, Isham
Bocock, John
Bucknall, Thomas
Barnett, Walter
Blankenship, Lodewick, Sr.; Lodewick, Jr.
Bracher, Mary
Bailey, William-Treble Tax
Bell, John
Bolling, James
Burns, John
Bailey, James
Barker, John
Barksdill, John; Henry
Bradbury, Henry
Baughan, Aris
Byrd, Samuel
Barker, John
Baughan, Reuben
Bristoe, Benjamin; Francis
Bailey, Carr
Barrett, William
Bitten, Anthony
Barrett, William
Burner, Charles
Baker, Joseph
Baughan, Henry
Bradberry, Joseph
Briscoe, John
Bolling, John; Christopher, Senr.
Barnard, Charles
Barker, Michael
Brammer, John
Birks, William; Rowland
Burks, Joseph-Treble Tax
Bryant, Josiah
Burnett, Jeremiah

Bays, William
Blair, Joseph
Bays, Peter, Sr.-Treble Tax; Peter, Jr.
Baker, John; Edward; Richard
Brammer, Burgess
Blackley, Acquilla
Blevins, Willoughby
Breeding, William
Britton, John-Montgomery
Brown, William(2); John
Boatman, Richard
Bolling, William; James
Bell, Henry
Booth, John
Burch, John, Jr.; John, Senr.
Burch, Jarrett
Blagg, John
Barnett, William, Esqr.
Bartlett, Frederick
Britton, George
Brillaman, Daniel
Birch, Daniel
Butterworth Orphans-Bedford
Bush, Thomas
Bearshears, Philip, Senr.
Blevins, William, Jr.; William, Senr.; John; Dillon
Bouldin, Joseph
Bolling, John
Bailey, Thomas
Bolling, Archibald
Bershears, Phillip, Jun.; Robert
Burns, Charles; Samuel
Bunch, David
Brown, William; Augustine
Barrett, Miles; John; Francis
Baker, Robert
Barton, William
Buzzard, Phillip
Burge, Woody
Burdge, Alexander
Belcher, Thomas
Barrott, Robert (Robt. Stockton to pay)
Brannum, William
Bennett, Richard; James
Bowman, Peter, Jr.
Bolling, John, Senr.; John, Junr.
Baker, Nicholas
Bartlett, Nathan
Blanchett, Peter
Bartlett, John
Bird, Abraham, Senr.
Biggs, Henry
Bowman, Robert; Robert, Junr; John

Birks, John

Cook, William, Esq.
Carter, Bailey
Choat, Isham; Edward, Jr.;
  Edward; Austin
Callaway, Early & Co.; &
  Early; James
Carter, Daniel
Cummings, Thomas
Carter, Joseph-Treble Tax
Choat, Sabrit
Coolley, James
Connor, William
Clarketon(?), David
Craighead, Peter
Callaway, James
Chandler, Benjamin
Cook, Benjamin, Jr.
Chandler, John
Choice, Tully, Senr.
Cockerham, William
Cowden, William
Clay, William
Cowden, James
Camp, John
Cockerham, Abner
Coates, Jessee
Clark, John; Spencer
Chitwood, John
Choice, Tully; William
Cunningham, John
Cantwell, Abednigo
Carter, Baynes; James
Crouch, John, Senr.; John,
  Jr.-Treble Tax
Copland, Richard; Peter
Cooper, Joseph
Collier, Charles
Cave, Robert
Cooper, John; Thomas
Coggin, William
Chesterton, John
Coasey, James
Cox, William
Collier, Richard
Coutts, Patrick
Casay, Daniel
Crowley, Elizabeth
Chiles, Henry
Collier, John
Conley, Enoch
Crouch, John, Junr.; Joseph;
  John, Jr.
Clement, Mathew
Collier, John
Coleman, Williamson-Dinwiddie
Cox, James
Connelly, William
Cox, Francis; John
Cloud, William
Carroll, Judith
Crowley, John

Cox, Anthony
Couch, Mary
Combs, John
Cox, Tolliver; William
Cobler, Frederick; Thomas
Cockram, Sarah
Cocram, Edward
Chandler, Jessee
Collier, Thomas
Cox, Russell; Charles
Collier, John
Cantwell, John
Critz, Frederick; Hamon,
  Senr.
Collier, Richard
Carter, George
Chisu, Elijah
Cammeron, John
Cannon, Benjamin
Cloway, Michael
Coats, John
Cantwell, Mary
Critz, Hamon, Junr.
Cummins, Benjamin
Cloud, Joseph
Cox, Phillip; Jacob; John
Cantwell, Adam
Cloud, Jason
Cheek, Jessee
Check, William; Richard,
  Senr.
Creed, Elijah
Carlin, Daniel
Cox, Jasper
Carrell, Cornelius
Cannon, Samuel
Condley, John-Treble Tax
Cox, Benjamin; Samuel;
  John-800 acres in Pitts-
  ylvania Co.

Dewuse, Lewis
Davis, Jonathan
Dunn, William
Davis, William; Lewis
Dillingham, Joshua
Davis, Soloman
Duvall, Benjamin
Dillingham, William;
  William, Jr.
Daughton, John
Davis, Joseph
Doggett, Miller
Davis, John
Dillard, James
Dunn, Michael
Dillon, Samuel
Dillingham, John
Dunlap, Henry
Daniel, George
Dillon, Henry
Dillingham, Michael
Dodson, William

Davis, William
Denny, James
Dunway(?), Cornelius
Dolozer, Edward
Daniel, Reuben
Donelson, Isaac
Doyal, John
Delozer, Jessee
Dykes, James
Darnold, Nicholas
Durram, James
Dunn, Richard
Durram, Thomas
Dickerson, John (Surveyor)
Dunn, Waters, Senr; Waters, Junr.
Dillinder, Jacob
Dobbs, John
Danham, Charles
Dooley, Thomas
Dodson, Charles
Dillard, John
Derham, Gregory
Dodson, Lambath
Dunkin, Martin
Deakins, William
Duinberry, Henry
Dickerson, James
Depriest, Tabitha
Denson, William
Daniel, William
Donthan, Elijah
Davison, William, Senr.; William

Emit, Richard
Evins, William
Ellis, Joseph
Evins, Thomas
Early, John
Edmundson, Richard; Humphry
Estes, Elisha, Senr.; Joel; Bottom; Elisha, Jr.; Elisha - Benbow
Edwards, Abel
Ellis, John
Edwards, Arthur
Estes, Elisha - 1 Mill; William
Echolls, Abner
Elkins, Nathaniel; James; Ralph; James
Earls, Thomas
Edwards, Thomas
Elliott, George
Edwards, James; William
East, William
Edwards, William, Jr.; Thomas, Junr; Edmund
Executors of James Hicks
Edwards, Isham
East, John
Edwards, James, Junr.
Epperson, Joseph, Senr.

Epperson, Joseph, Junr.
East. James
Eades, Charles; Abraham
Evans, George

Farguson, John
Fox, Samuel
Fewston, John
Farguson, John-Nichoas's Creek; John, Jr.; William
Frazer, Robert
Foster, Charles
Farrell, John
Foley, Luke; Bartholomew
Flowers, Thomas
Fancher, Richard
Franklin, Abraham
Finch, John; Charles
Farris, William
Farguson, Joseph
Fenit, Thomas
Fontaine, John
Franklin, George
Fulkerson, Frederick
French, William
France, Peter; Mary
Finn, William
Fletcher, John
Frazer, Abraham
Fitzgerald, Frederick
France, Henry
Finn, Daniel-Treble Tax
Fee, Thomas-Treble Tax; William-Treble Tax
Flood, Comfort
Fee, Thomas, Jr.-Treble Tax
Fulkerson, James
Fortner, William, Senr.

Grimmit, Robert
Gearhart, Peter
Grimmit, John
Graypeal, Peter-Treb. Tax
Greer, Shadrick-Treb. Tax
Grayham, Archibald
Greer, Moses; James; Thomas; William-Treb. Tax
Gwilliams, Edgcomb
Grimmit, Robert
Ginkins, Lewis; William
Graves, William, Senr.; David
Greer, William; Acquilla
Goff, John
Gilliam, Peter
Graves, William, Jr.
Gordon, Archibald
Garner, Thomas
Goode, John
Going, John
Goodin, Joseph
Gardner, William
Gibson, Randolph; Archibald

Goff, Thomas
Green, John-Treb. Tax; James
Grayham, Francis
Gravely, Joseph; John-Treb. Tax
Garner, Thomas
Griggs, John
Garland, Elizabeth
Golsby, Daniel
Gardner, William
Gilley, Francis, Junr; Charles; Richard
Gray, Samuel
Gates, Samuel
Going, Jessee
Groging, John
Gilley, Francis, Senr.
Goodman, Joseph
George, William; John
Gilliam, Deverix
Gooch, Jones
Gillington, John
Grisham, John
Gazaway, Thomas
Gooch, Nathan
Green, William
Gates, James
Going, John
Golding, Jacob
Going, James; David
Gibson, Thomas
Gooch, Rachell
Gibson, Thomas, Jr.

Holliday, Robert
Hargar, John
Hale, Joseph
Hoff, Peter
Houser, Jasper
Hedges, Catareah
Hiland, James
Hill, Swinfield; Violet; Mary; Ruth
Hogard, James
Hale, Joseph-Treble Tax
Hodges, Robert
Holcomb, Grymes
Hancock, Thomas
Hairston, Robert
Hale, Thomas, Capt.
Hammon, William
Hubbard, Eusebas
Hanes, George
Hale, Lewis
Haynes, John; Henry, Jr.; Henry, Senr.
Huggen, Luke
Hogen, William
Haynes, William
Hogin, Micajah
Hutchinson, Paul; William
Heard, Thomas
Hodges, William, Senr.
Hall, Lamford

Hodges, Josiah
Hooker, Mary
Hodges, William, Jr.; Isham
Hubbard, Mary
Huckaby, Robert; John
Hall, Jessee; Isham
Hickerson, Thomas
Heard, Jessee; George; William; Stephen; John
Holt, Ambrose
Hall, William
Hartwell, John
Hickman, Peter
Hollingsworth, Thomas
Haley, David
Hamilton, Mary; George
Hubbard, Harrison
Harris, Henry
Heard, John; William, Jr.
Hickey, John-Treb. Taxed
Harmer & King
Hunter, Alexander; William
Hollinsworth, William
Hick, James - Geo. Hamilton to pay
Hord, Mordicai
Hairston, George
Hughes, Blackmore
Handy, John
Hall, Nathan; John
Harbour, Easias; Joel
Harris, Peter
Hurt, Joseph
Hoff, Samuel; Thomas
Hilton, Samuel
Hubbard, Benjamin; Thomas
Hibbert, Charles
Harrison, Henry
Henderson, John; Thomas
Hulett, Martin
Henry, Patrick, Esq.
Hopper, Thomas
Hill, Thomas - Breeches
Hairston, Peter (omitted)
Hoskins, William
Harbour, David; Joyce
Holt, Richard
Hambleton, Thomas
Hall, John
Harbour, Elisha
Hammons, Joseph
Hardeman, John; William
Hays, William
Hambrick, Nimrod
Harmer, John - Marrowbone
Hoard, Mordicai
Hughes, Archaleus, Col.
Hawkins, William
Halbert, William
Hooker, Robert, Junr; Robert, Senr.
Hudson, Peter
Hinton, William

Hamilton, Thomas
Hutchinson, Richard
Holder, John
Hilton, James; Solomon
Hooker, John
Humphry, Morris-Treb. Tax
Hensely, Benjamin - Capt.
Hudson, Obediah
Hensley, Benjamin-Treb. Tax
Hickumbottom, William
Howell, Paul
Hudspeth, William
Hammon, John
Holstonpack, Derick
Hawks, John; William
Hardwick, Thomas
Holt, Phillip
Hill, Thomas
Herrington, John; James
Hall, John
Hanby, Jonathan

Innes, Hugh
Ingram, James; John
Ison, John; William; Charles;
  Jonathan; James
Ivie, Howell; Elisha
Innes, Hugh - 800 acres-same

Jones, Thomas, Junr.; Isaac
  Abraham; Henry; John;
  Robert, Junr.; Robert,
  Senr.; Thomas, Capt.
Jamison, John
Jones, Ambrose, Junr.; Ambrose,
  Senr.; William-Reed Creek
Jamison, Thomas
Jordan, Hezekiah
Jones, Thomas
Johnson, William
James, Jamey; John
Johnson, Hudson-Treb. Tax
Jones, John, Senr.; John, Junr.-
  Kentucky; George
Jarvis, Alexander
Jackson, Daniel
Johnson, Samuel
Jamison, William; John
Jones, Daniel
Jordan, Samuel
Johnson, James
Jamison, Thomas
Joyce, Alexander
Jonnakin, John
Johnson, Noble
Jones, William
Jennings, Miles
Jones, Thomas
Johnson, Jacob-Treb. Tax
Joyce, John-525 acres from
  Pittsylvania

Kelly, William

Keel, Richard
Kimmings, James
Keel, James; John
Kelly, Andrew; William, Jr.
Kearby, Joseph; Jessee;
  Jessee-Pigg River; John;
  David
Keen, William; John; Elisha
King, Walter-Great Britian;
  Joseph
Kitchen, William
Kogar, John
Kindrick, John
Kearby, Richard
Kogar, Nicholas
Kimzey, Benjamin, Jr.
King, Nathaniel
Kennady, William
King, Stephen
Kelly, John
King, John
Kinton, Thomas
Kindrick, Preston
King, Walter - Marrowbone
Kesire, Lodwick
Ketchum, Nathaniel
Kogar, Jacob; Henry
Keeton, William
Kerney, Gilbert

Lee, Stephen
Levisey, Thomas; George
Lewis, Hezekiah
Law, John, Senr.
Long, William
Law, Henry; William;
  Nathaniel
Lutterall, Samuel
Lewis, Thomas
Law, John
Lumsden, John, Junr.; John,
  Senr.
Lee, Joshua-Treb. Tax;
  Zadock; John
Lyne, Edmund; Henry
Lamb, Walter
Loyd, John; James
Loyall, Joseph-Brunswick
Lovell, William
Lomax, Randolph, Harmer &
  King
Linear, Samuel
Lucas, John
Lanier, David
Lovell, Daniel
Leak, Thomas
Linch, William
Lawson, David; William;
  Moreman
Leak, Peter
Lankford, Robert
Linch, James
Lyon, James

Lawson, William
Lowe, Thomas
Loving, Mary
Lindsey, John
Lawson, Jonas
Letcher, William
Landers, Benjamin

Moseley, Mordicai
Murphy, John
Manifee, Wm. Sr., Treb. Tax
Musgrove, Samuel
Miller, William
Middleton, John
Miller, Joseph; Thomas
Martin, John
Mullins, William
McGee, Holden
Martin, Hugh; James
Musteen, Jean
McGlaughlin, John
McGuire, Alazany
McCoy, Richard
Mullins, John
Mason, Robert
Mattocks, Michael
Moore, John
Menifee, John; William, Jr.
Maxey, Walter
Major, James
McKinsey, Aaron
Milam, Samuel
Mason, William-Treb. Tax
Moore, Garrett
McKinsey, Kinney
Murphy, James
McBride, Patrick
Meredith, Junor
McWilliams, Hugh
Matlock, David
Mullins, William
McCraw, Jacob
Meredith, Bradley-Treb. Tax
Mitchell, James
McCraw, William
Martin, Brice
McDonald, Isaac
McBride, James
Murrell, Thomas; Thomas (long)
Morrow, Thomas
McAlexander, William
McPeak, Ezekiel; James; William
Morrison, Thomas
Mabry, George
Mayo, Valentine
Musick, Elexores
McKiney, John
McAdowe, Ann
McCuffey, Ephraim
Mitchell, Robert; William; John
Minter, John

Murrell, Jeffery-Treb. Tax
Mastes, Jarrett
Morton, James
Milton, James
Malin, John
Miller, John
Morgan, John
McBride, Daniel
Marshall, Thomas
Mays, David; Sherwood
Moore, Benjamin
Moseley, Thomas
Mannin, Davis; Henry
Moore, William
McKain, Hugh
McGee, John
McKain, Thomas
Major, John
Meredith, James
Martin, Joseph
McKain, Alexander
Marr, John
Mays, Henry; Abraham
Mannin, John; Samuel
Maxey, Sampson
Minnis, John
Murphy, William
Mill's Order (Matrimony)
Miller, John
Murry, Thomas
Mathews, John
Mattinley, Richard
Midcalf, Nathan
Mankins, James
Moore, Chatten
McMillion, Andrew
Midkeff, Thomas
May, James; John
Moore, Rhodham
McGown, John, Senr.-Treb. Tax; John, Jr.; David; Samuel
McConway, John
Mitchell, James-tax Pittsyl.

Nelson, William
Nowland, George
Noe, Prior-Treb. Tax; John, Senr.; John, Jr.
Norris, John
Nunn, Ingram; Thomas
Noe, Samuel
Neavill, John
Newport, Richard
Newton, Richard
Newgant, Ludley
Northcutt, John
Nash, Marvel
Nance, Ruben; John
Nelson, Thomas
Newman, Joseph; Daniel; John
Nicholls, John

Neal, Susannah

Oliver, James
Oldham, John; James
Oneil, Bazel
Owen, John
Oakley, Richard; Thomas, Senr.; Thomas, Jr.; James
Oldham, Mary; Thomas
Oliver, James-tax from Pittsa.

Prilliman, Jacob
Phelps, Solomon
Pepes (Piper), Joseph
Parrot, Thorp
Parker, John
Prilliman, Jacob, Jr.-Treb. Tax
Patterson, Samuel
Peck, Jonathan; George
Peirson, Joseph
Peck, David
Potter, Benjamin; Lewis
Powell, Robert
Prewitt, David, Senr.
Prewit, David, Jr.; Elijah
Pinkard, John
Prunty, Thomas; James
Perryman, Richard
Patterson, Samuel
Prunty, Robert
Packsood, Samuel; Richard
Perryman, Robert
Polley, Edward
Parsley, Thomas; John
Palfrey, John
Philpott, John
Posey, Humphry
Penn, Abraham
Parsley, Richard
Pewsey, Robert
Peregoy, Edward
Peck, Abel
Prator, Jonathan; Archibald
Prater, Ninian
Prator, William
Polson, Andrew
Poteet, James
Posey, Francis
Pyrtle, John
Payne, Reubeen
Perkins, Nicholas
Pedigo, Robert
Parry, Thomas
Potter, Thomas
Price, Joseph
Pace, John
Payne, Josiah; Thomas; John, Senr.
Pratley, James
Payne, Abraham
Pool, George; Micajah
Payne, John, Junr.
Parker, Samuel

Polley, John
Prater, Minar
Pilgrim, Amos
Poore, George, Junr.; William
Pullim, John
Pilgrim, Michael
Parr, John, Junr; John, Senr.
Poore, George, Senr.
Parr, Henry
Pilgram, Amos
Pigg, James
Patterson, Jarrett
Paxton, Joseph
Pace, John-tax from Pittsylva.
Peak, George - same

Ramsey, John
Rentfro, James
Reel, Michael; Andrew
Richardson, Stanhope
Roads, Christian
Ross, Daniel
Ramsey, George
Richards, Edward
Rentfro, Joshua
Roberts, Thomas
Reuball, Owen
Ryan, Darby
Roach, John
Reeves, Frederick
Richardson, Amons, Senr.
Raley, Phillip
Ryan, William
Ringo, Cornelius
Richardson, John
Randall, Samuel
Ross, David
Roberson, Richard
Richardson, Amos, Jr.
Roberson, John; Thomas, Jr.; Thomas
Richardson, Daniel
Richmond, John; William
Reed, William
Ringo, Stephen; John
Rowland, Baldwin; John, Senr.
Redd, John
Reeves, George
Rowland, Michael
Reynolds, Richard; James
Royall, John
Ratliff, Silas; John; Richard
Rentfro, William
Radford, John
Rich, John; William
Reynolds, Richard, Senr.; Spencer; Richard, Jr.; George

Rigar, Jacob
Rice, William
Reynolds, John
Rutter, Abraham
Roach, John
Rea, James, Senr.; William
Richardson, John
Roberts, James-Pittsylva.
Rice, John - same
Rea, Andrew
Roberson, Archd.
Ramey, John
Rice, Benjamin; William
Rowland, George
Rea, James, Junr.
Ramey, Daniel
Ryan, Phillip
Rowland, John
Rea, John
Roberson, William; Wm. -
  (King & Queen)
Roberts, Jos. Executors
Right, Samuel
Roberts, William; James
Redman, James-Treb. Tax;
  Rhoda
Reynolds, Bartlett
Ridle, John
Rice, Daniel
Russell, John
Rice, Spencer
Reynolds, John; Moses;
  Susannah
Rogers, David; George
Rowgin, Hugh
Ray, Thomas
Royalty, Isham
Rice, William
Richards, Thomas
Rowles, Christopher
Rentfro, John

Sinter, Stephen-tax from Pittsyl.
Saunders, Peter
Spangler, Daniel
Sheridan, Phillip
Stout, Joseph-Treb. Tax; Samuel
Stanley, William
Smith, Daniel
Stanley, John; Robert
Stewart, James, Senr; James, Jr.
Stanley, Joseph
Stewart, David
Stover, Jacob
Standefore, James; William;
  Luke; James, Jr.
Stanton, John; Robert
Stanley, William, Junr; Richard
Smith, Thomas; John
Shockley, Levi
Strange, James
Swanson, William, Jr.;
  William, Senr.; John

Southerland, Samuel
Sousberry, Jeremiah
Senter, Stephen
Spaulden, Thomas
Street, Anthony-Lunenberg
Stegall, William-Halifax Co.
Shumate, Daniel
Simpson, Baxter
Stewart, John
Standefore, Israel
Stevens, John; William
Swanson, Nathan
Stamps, John
Scrasey, Robert
Simms, Ignatious
Stokes, John; George
Smallman, John
Sumpter, George
Scruggs, Julius
Sumpter, Henry
Smith, Daniel
Salmon, John
Street, Joseph
Small, Jean; Mathew; John
Stinnett, Benjamin
Smith, John
Salmon, Rowland
Sneed, John
Slatter, Joseph
Short, James
Stewart, William; John
Swann, Jonathan
Smith, Edward
Scoggins, Humphrey
Stephens, William
Street, Samuel
Stephens, John
Scales, Joseph
Stephens, Sampson (?);
  William-Treble Tax
Smith, Thomas; John
Stallings, Jacob
Samms, William, Senr.;
  William, Jr.
Sandford, John
Scoggins, George
Samms, John
Simmons, John
Smith, Thomas
Sinkler, Charles
Shelton, Azariah; James;
  Ralph; Eliphaz
Smith, Henry
Shelton, Palatiah
Ship, Josiah
Shrad, James
Stockton, Thomas; Agnes
Simmons, Zachariah
Sharp, William
Shelton, Jeremiah; James,
  Capt.; William
Spencer, James
Smith, Anthony; Bradley

Short, Henry
Smith, William
Sowell, Joseph
Sims, John
Scales, Nathaniel
Spencer, James, Senr.
Sims, Mathew; Bartlett; Sarah
Solomon, Drury
Shelton, John
Sturgeon, Ambrose-Treble Tax
Smith, Isaac; Josiah; Tadock;
  William, Junr.; Bartlett
Stewart, John, Senr.; James;
  John, Jr.
Solomon, Isham
Stewart, Edward
Smith, Munford; Randell;
  William

Turpin, James
Thompson, Sherwood
Terry, Thomas
Thompson, William
Thorp, William
Tarrant, Leonard
Turley, Peter
Tillason, Francis
Threlkeld, Thomas
Tate, Nathaniel; Robert; Henry
Turner, John
Thomas, Phillip
Turner, William; Shadrack;
  Josiah; John (Smith River)
Thomas, Charles
Tenison, Zaphaniah
Tittle, Anthony; John
Tension, Jessee
Turnly, John
Tarrant, James
Tankersly, John; Richard
Tarrant, Mary; Samuel; John
Tackett, William
Troup, Jacob
Thornton, Luke
Thompson, William-Treble Tax
Tunstall, William
Taylor, James; George
Torbourn, Elinor
Terrell, William
Taylor, James; William; George
Thomas, Augustine
Thompson, James
Tatum, Edward; Jessee

Underwood; Samuell

Vardeman, Peter
Vincent, Henry; William
Varnell, Richard
Veall, Nathan
Vandegriff, Leonard, Senr.
Vandegrif, Jacob

Woods, Hugh
Warren, Thomas; Zachariah;
  Drury; William
Webb, Smith
Woods, John; Robert; Joseph
Wickings, Robert
Willis, Henry; Joseph; John
Webb, William; Henry
Walton, Robert (Callaway &
  Early to pay)
Walker, Joel
Wilks, John
Ward, Daviel
Woodall, John
Wooton, John
Webster, Joseph
Witt, John; William
Watson, John
Waller, George
Williams, James
Warrdin, Robert-Treb. Tax
Walden, Aaron
Williams, Elizabeth; John
Warren, Henry
Wheat, Benjamin
Wyatt, John
Watson, Robert
Wilson, Martha; Thomas;
  James; Moses; Daniel
Watson, Michael; Samuel;
  David
Wells, Mathew; John
Warwick, Jacob
Wilkinson, William
Webb, Merry
Walling, Elisha
Wellingham, Jessee
Witt, David
Williams, Joseph
Wilion, John - Pittsa.
Webb, Thomas; Morris
Willingham, John
Williams, Garriot
Webb, Elizabeth
Whaley, William
Webb, William
Wilson, William
Willis, John
Weatherspoon, William
Walker, Samuel
Willis, Thomas
Wilson, Harris
Witt, Jessee; John
Watson, John
Welch, Richard
Ward, Thomas
Watson, Robert
Watkins, George
Webb, Isham
Wonn(?), William

Young, John; William;
  Peter, Agnes; Ridley;

Young cont'd.: William; Daniel;
   Joshua

DEDUCT
Britton, John - Montgomery
Butterworth's Orphans - Bedford
Jones, John, Jr. - Kentucky
Loyall, Joseph - Brunswick
Roberts, James - Pittsylvania

Robertson, Wm.-King & Queen
Street, Anthony - Lunenburg
Wilson, John - Pittsylvania
Stegall, William - Halifax
Rice, John - Pittsylvania
Coleman, Williamston-Dinwiddie

September 13, 1779. Rec'd of the Commissioners of Henry County a copy of the foregoing list of Taxes on a pound rate which I promise to collect and account for Agreeable to an Act of Assembly in the case made and provided.
                              Signed:
                              John Salmon, Sh.
Wit:
   John Cox

At a meeting of the Commissioners of Henry County at the Courthouse of Henry County at the Courthouse on the 23rd of Sept. 1779, present Robert Hairston & John Dillard. The Estate of John Rentfro, one of the assessors is assessed agreeable to Law. The Tax of 1/gallon on Stephen Heards liquor taken off also on Peter Gilliams.
                              Robert Hairston
                              John Dillard

An alphabetical List of Tax in the County of Henry for raising a supply of money for the Service of the United States. Delivered to Archaleus Hughes, Esq., Sherif of the said County to collect, due the 20th day of February 1780.

Anthony, Joseph
Anderson, Armstead
Alexander, John (Matrimony)
Anglin, Joseph; Phillip
Allen, Fisher
Alexander, John, Sr.; William
Abbington, John; Bowles
Adkinson, Jesse
Adams, William; Richard; Joseph; Thomas
Arnold, Henry; William
Adams, Jacob
Allen, Samuel
Anthony, James
Adams, Thomas; Abraham; Jacob; William
Akin, James
Agg, Mathew
Acuff, John
Akins, Nicholas
Anderson, James; Peter; James
Alley, Nickolas
Adkinson, David; Jacob
Archer, William
Allen, John; George
Armstrong, James

Alexander, John, Jr.

Bush, Thomas
Bolling, John
Blevins, Dillion
Bell, Henry
Blevins, John
Burns, Samuel
Buckley, Samuel
Bunch, David
Bolling, Archilbald
Bouldin, Joseph
Blevins, William, Jr.; William, Sr.
Bailey, Thomas
Broshears, Phillip; Robert; Phillip, Senr.
Brown, Augustine
Bolt, John
Baher, Robert
Belcher, Thomas
Bush, Conrod
Buzzard, Phillip
Barrott, John
Burdge, Woody; Alexander
Bolling, William
Barton, William

Brannon, Benjamin
Barrott, Robert
Blaikey, George
Barnard, Charles; Abner
Brammer, John; James
Birks, John; Rowland
Bryant, Josiah
Bays, William; Peter
Blair, Joseph
Bays, Peter, Jr.
Baker, John; Richard
Blackley, Acquilla
Blevins, Willoughby
Breeding, William
Barrington, Joseph
Barker, Michael
Birke, William
Bedford, Thomas
Byrd, John
Briscoe, John
Bradberry, Joseph
Bolling, Christopher, Senr.
Briscoe, George
Baker, James
Bolling, Samuel
Baughan, Aris; Reuben
Burnett, Charles
Baughan, Henry
Barksdale, John; Henry
Barker, John; John (Smith River)
Byrd, Samuel
Bradberry, Henry
Bitting, Anthony
Baker, William
Bristoe, Benjamin; Francis
Baker, Joseph
Bailey, William
Burns, John
Bolling, James
Butler, William
Birch, John, Senr.; John, Jr.
Blagge, John
Booth, John
Birch, Jarrett
Boahanan, Richard
Bolling, Joseph; James; William
Brown, William; Daniel
Brittain, George
Brown, William (Weaver)
Bernard, William
Bolton, Robert; Thomas
Bennet, William
Brock, Joshua
Bernard, Waller
Blassingham, Phillip
Busknall, Thomas
Burton, Seth
Belcher, Isham
Blankenship, Lodewick; Isham
Bernard, Nathan
Bryant, James
Bocock, John

Baugan, Phillip
Beckler, David
Beck, Paul
Barton, Isaac; David
Bates, John
Bartee, William
Bowles, George
Bell, William; John
Bybee, Sherwood; John
Briant, John
Bohannan, William
Boyd, William
Blanchell, Peter
Baxter, John
Bartlett, John
Byrd, Abraham
Beamer, Peter
Burks, John; Rowland
Byrd, Elisha
Bennett, Richard; John
Bolling, John, Senr.
Bowman, Robert; Peter, Robert, Jr.

Chandler, Jessee
Cookesham, Edward
Currey, John
Cox, Toliver; William
Cobler, Thomas; Frederick
Cox, Russell; Charles
Cannon, John
Cloe, Michael
Colley, John
Cannon, Benjamin
Camron, Joseph
Collier, John
Coates, John
Critz, Hammon, Senr.; Hamon, Jr.
Collier, Richard
Carter, George
Commains, Benjamin
Cummins, Malakiah
Clark, Joseph
Cantwell, John
Casey, Daniel
Chiles, Henry
Collier, William
Conley, Enoch
Copland, Peter
Cooper, Joseph
Carter, Baynes
Crouch, John
Charles, James
Copland, Richard
Carter, Josiah
Cave, Robert
Casteel, Abednigo
Chadwell, David
Crouch, John, Jr.
Cunningham, John
Cooper, John; Thomas
Casey, James

Collier, Richard
Cloud, Jason
Caiton, Jacob
Cox, Anthony; John
Combs, John
Crouch, John, Senr.; John, Jr.; Joseph
Cox, Francis
Cornwell, Richard
Cornnell, William
Cox, James
Connray, John
Conner, John
Collier, John
Clarkson, David
Craghead, Peter
Camp, John
Clay, William
Cowden, James
Chambers, William
Clay, Jessee
Cockerham, Abner
Clark, Spencer
Cook, Benjamin
Choice, Tully, Senr.; William, Tully
Cowden, William
Chandler, Benjamin
Choat, Labet
Chimans, James
Choat, Isham
Cooley, James
Choat, Edward; Edward, Jr.; Augustine
Cassot, Thomas
Commings, Thomas
Clack, John
Callaway & Early
Conner, William
Carter, Joseph; Bailey
Coates, Jessee
Cook, William
Callaway, James
Cox, Mathew
Creed, Elijah
Cannon, Samuel
Carter, Daniel
Cassell, Cronelius
Cox, Benjamin
Cook, Jester
Cheek, William
Cox, John
Cloud, Isaac
Cantwell, Adam
Cheek, Willis
Commer, James
Couchery, William
Cheek, Jessee
Cox, Samuel

Dunn, Waters, Senr.
Dobbs, John
Dunn, Waters, Jr.

Dooley, Thomas
Dickins, Richard
Duncan, Martin
Durham, Gregory
Dillard, John
Deuzenberry, Henry
Dodson, Charles
Dickerson, James
Donathan, Nelson
Deney, James
Dewies, Cornilius
Dillion, Henry
Dunlap, Henry
Dillingham, Michael; John
Dillion, Benjamin
Dodson, William
Donelson, Isaac
Daniel, Reuben
Dickerson, Thompson
Darnold, Nickolas
Davis, John
Dial, John
Dykes, James
Dunn, Richard
Dunam, James
Dunn, Michael
Davis, Nathan; Soloman
Dillion, James; Samuel
Davis, John
Dodson, Lamboth
Davey, Isaac
Dillard, James
Doughton, John
Dickenson, John
Davis, Joseph
Dillingham, Joshua; William; William, Jr.
Davis, Jonathan; Solomon
Duval, Benjamin
Davis, William; Lewis
Duvall, Lewis
Dolazer, Edward
Daniel, William
Denison, William
Donathan, William; Elijah
Davison, William

East, John
Elliott, George
East, William
Edwards, James; William; James; Isham; Thomas, Jr.; Edmund
East, James
Erste, Miller
Ecton, James
Eckolls, Abner
Elkins, Nathaniel; James; William; Ralph
Estes, William
Evans, Amos
Elkins, James; Ralph
Earls, Thomas

Edwards, Thomas
Ellis, John
Edwards, Abel; Arthur
Estes, Elisha, Senr.; Joel;
  Elisha (Benbo); Elisha,
  Jr.; Bottom
Edmundson, Richard; Humphry
Easley, John
Ellis, Joseph
Evans, William; Thomas
Eubank, William
Earley, Joseph
Evans, George
Eades, Abraham

Farguson, Joseph
Finch, Charles
Farris, William
Franklin, George
Fontaine, John
France, Mary
Fulkerson, Frederick
French, William
Fee, Thomas; William
Fain, William
France, Henry; Peter
Fletcher, John
Fain, Daniel
Farrell, John
Foley, Luke; Bartlett
Fencher, Richard
Flowers, Thomas
Foster, Charles
Fuller, Brittain
Fuqua, James (for Guy Smith)
Fletcher, Joseph
Fox, Samuel
Frazer, Robert
Fuson, John
Farguson, John; John, Sr.;
  John; William
Frazer, Abraham
Fisher, Jabus
Forkner, William

George, William; John
Gray, Samuel
Gates, Samuel
Graves, William
Goodman, Joseph
Golesby, Daniel
Gallemore, Samuel
Going, Jessee
Gilley, Francis, Senr.
Gardner, William
Gilley, Francis, Jr.; Charles;
  Dick
Gilliam, Deverix
Grisham, John, Senr.
Gazaway, Thomas
Going, David; John; James
Gates, William
Gardner, William (Smith River)

Gibson, Randolph; Richard;
  James; John
Green, John; James
Grayham, Francis
Gofs, Thomas
Godard, James
Going, John
Gossett, John
Garner, Thomas
Goodwin, Joseph
Griggs, John
Graveley, Joseph
Gordon, Archibald
Graves, William, Senr.;
  William
Greer, Aquilla
Goff, John
Gilliam, Peter
Gregpeel, Peter
Greer, Moses; James; Moses;
  Shadrick; William
Gwilliams, Edgcomb
Grayham, Archioald
Grimmit, Robert
Gravet, Obediah
Grammit, Robert
Grearheart, John
Greer, Uriah
Gossett, John
Griffin, William
Grymes, John
Garrot, Benjamin; Joseph

Hardeman, John; William
Hamilton, Thomas
Holt, John
Hambrick, Nimrod
Holt, Richard
Harbour, Elisha
Hayse, William
Hamilton, Samuel
Holt, Edmund
Hamilton, Thomas
Hooker, John; Robert
Hutchinson, Richard
Hughes, Archaleus
Hill, Manning
Hudson, Peter
Hilton, James
Helton, Soloman
Halbert, William
Hall, John
Hudson, Joshua
Holder, John
Hairston, Robert
Hughes, Blackmore
Handy, John
Hairston, Robert
Hughes, Blackmore
Handy, John
Hall, Nathan; John
Harbour, Esaias; Joel
Hurt, Joseph

Harris, Peter
Hoff, Samuel; Thomas
Hilton, Samuel; John; Newman; Jessee
Hubbard, Benjamin; Thomas
Hibberts, Charles
Hairston, George
Hord, Mordecai
Hardy, Joseph
Hubbard, Harrison
Hickman, Peter
Hamilton, George
Heard, William, Senr.; John
Harris, Henry
Heard, William
Hunter, Alexander
Hatcher, Archablad
Hollinsworth, William, Senr.; Thomas
Hunter, William
Hickey, John
Hailey, David
Harris, William (a free negro)
Henry, Patrick, Esq.
Hopper, Thomas
Hall, Merry
Haynes, George; Henry, Jr.; William
Hartwell, John
Hall, William; Isham; Lansford; Jessee
Heard, Jessee; George; Stephen; John; Thomas
Holt, Ambrose
Haynes, Henry, Senr.
Hodges, Isham; William
Hutchenson, Peter
Hutchinson, Ambrose; Paul; Phillip
Hubbard, Eusebus
Hogins, William
Hickerson, Thomas
Hodges, Josiah
Hairston, Robert
Holcomb, Grymes
Houser, Jasper
Holliday, Robert
Hogard, James
Harger, John
Hodges, Robert
Hill, Swinfield
Hale, Joseph; Thomas; Joseph, Jr.
Hoff, Peter
Hale, Thomas, Capt.
Hancock, John
Henders, John
Hall, Thomas
Henderson, John; Thomas
Hill, Thomas
Hairston, Peter
Humphreys, Morriss
Hammons, John

Hamilton, Thomas
Herrington, James
Hedspeth, William
Hardick, Thomas
Hawlsted, James
Holt, Phillip
Harrison, Henry
Holder, John; Lewis
Hawkes, John
Hill, Thomas
Holsenback, Derick
Hall, John
Harrington, John
Hickumbottom, William
Hudson, Obediah
Hensley, Benjamin, Capt.; John
Howell, Paul
Hensley, Benjamin, Jr.; Benjamin, Sr.
Hanby, Jonathan

Ivey, Howell
Ingram, James; John
Ion (?), William
Ison, Charles; Jonathan; James
Innes, Hugh
Ivey, Elisha

Jamison, Thomas
Journican, John
Johnson, James
Jennings, Miles
Jones, William; Thomas
Johnson, William; Hudson
James, Jamey; John
Jones, John; George
Jarvis, Alexander
Jones, Ambrose; Thomas; Richard
Jordon, Hezekiah; Soloman
Jamison, John; Thomas; William
Jones, Daniel
Jenkins, Lewis; William
Jamison, John
Jones, Thomas
Joyce, Alexander
Jones, Thomas, Jr.; Robert; Robert, Jr.; John; Henry; Abraham; Isaac
Johnson, Jacob
Johns, John

King, John
Kendrick, Preston
Kington, Francis
Koger, Jacob
Keaton, Joseph
Koger, Henry
Ketcham, Nathaniel
Keaton, William

Koger, John
Kearby, Richard
Kelly, Barnabas
Kinzey, Benjamin
Kennady, William
Kitching, William; John
King, Joseph
Kelley, John
Kearby, David
Kesterton, John
King, Stephen
Kearby, Jessee
Keen, Elisha
Kearby, Jessee; Josiah; Francis
Keen, John
Kittinger, Jacob
Keel, John
Kelley, William; Andrew; John; William; Michael
Kezziah, Lodewick

Lanier, David; Samuel
Leak, Thomas
Lovell, Daniel; William
Linch, William
Lindsay, John
Leak, Peter
Linch, James
Lawson, David; William; William (Big Billey)
Lyon, James
Lawson, John; David; Jonas
Lyon, Stephen
Lyne, Henry; Edmund
Lee, Tadock; John
Loyd, John; James; George
Long, William
Luttrell, Samuel
Lewis, Joseph
Law, John, Senr.; Jessee; Nathaniel; John, Jr.
Lumeden, John
Lee, Joshua; Stephen
Livesey, Thomas; George
Lewis, Hezekiah
Letcher, William
Launders, Benjamin

Moore, William
McGee, John
McKain, Alexander
Major, John
Mays, Henry; David
McKain, Thomas
Manning, John; Henry; Davis
Meredith, James
Mills, William
Moore, Benjamin
Meredith, David
Mays, Sherwood
Manley, Thomas
Martin, Joseph

Maxey, Walter
Morriss, John
Maxey, Sampson
Murphy, William
Mays, Abraham
May, James
Marshall, William
Marlow, Matt
Moore, Chatten
Morriss, Joseph; Samuel
McMillion, Andrew
Mathews, John
Miller, John
Massey, Thomas
Mankins, James
Medkiff, Thomas; Nathan; Jacob
Medkiff, James
Marr, John
McDonald, Isaac
McBride, James
Murrell, Thomas; Thomas (Long); Richard
Marrow, Thomas
McAlexander, William
McPeak, James; Ezekial
Morrison, Thomas
Mabry, George
McGuffey, Ephraim
Mayo, Valentine
Musick, Elexus; Jonathan
Mullins, Mathew
Martin, Brice
Meredith, Samuel; Junor; Bradley
Mann, John (a free negro)
McCraw, Jacob
Mitchell, James
Mason, William
McDonald, Michael
McKinzey, Kinney
Mullins, William; Ambrose; Richard
Matlock, David
Moor, Gassatt
McWilliams, Hugh
Mitchell, Ralph
Murphy, James
McCraw, William
Morgan, John
Mitchell, Robert; William
Morton, James
Minter, John
Moseley, Joseph
Mitchell, John
Masters, James
Marsters, Jarrett
Malins, John
Milton, James
Miller, John; William
McBride, Daniel
Milam, Samuel
Major, James

Mavity, William
Morling, Stephen
Macquier, Allege
McLaughlin, John
Musteen, William
McGee, Holden
Martin, Hugh; John
Mason, Robert
Martin, James
Manifee, William; William, Jr.
Moore, John
Moseley, Mordicai
McCoye, William; Richard; Walter
Mullins, William; John
Miller, Joseph
McGown, Samuel; David; John; Andrew; Alexander
Mitchell, William
Mattinley, Walter

Nelson, Thomas
Newman, Joseph; John; Daniel
Noe, Samuel
Neavell, John
Noe, John, Senr.; John
Nunn, Thomas
Norriss, John
Nunn, Ingram
Norris, Gilbert
Newport, Richard
Nance, Reuben; John
Nelson, William
Naufsinger, John

Oakley, Thomas; Thomas, Jr.; James; Richard
Owen, John
Oldham, Thomas
Oneal, Bazel
Oliver, James
Oldham, John, Senr.; John, Jr.; James
O'Briant, Dennis
O'Kerman, Nickolas

Payne, John; Josiah
Pool, George; Micajah
Price, Joseph
Payne, Abraham
Parsley, Thomas
Payne, Reuben
Pace, John
Prater, Nehemiah
Patterson, Jarrett; Edward
Polley, John
Pilgrim, Amos
Pigg, James
Pilgrim, William
Parker, Samuel
Poor, George; George, Jr.
Poore, William
Pilgrim, Michael

Pulliam, John
Parr, John, Senr.; Henry; John, Jr.
Pilgrim, Thomas
Pewrey, Robert
Peck, John
Prater, Jonathan; William; Ninion; Archibald
Polson, Andrew
Poteet, James
Passey, Francis
Pursell, John
Packwood, Samuel; Richard
Perryman, Robert
Palfrey, John
Penn, Abraham
Parsley, Richard; John; Abraham
Pedigo, Robert
Pyrtle, John
Pierson, Robert
Prewitt, David, Senr.
Potter, Benjamin; Lewis
Powell, Robert
Prunty, Thomas
Prewit, David, Jr.
Pinkard, John
Potter, Thomas
Prunty, James
Pratt, Jonathan
Parker, John
Paunty, Robert
Prillaman, Jacob; Jacob, Jr.
Parrot, Thorp
Prilliman, John
Piper, Joseph; Jacob
Prilliman, Daniel
Peck, Jonathan
Pool, Thomas
Patterson, Samuel
Powell, Jojeway
Poston, Joseph; Andrew

Rowland, George
Richardson, John
Ray, Andrew
Rea, James, Jr.
Rowland, John
Ramey, Daniel
Ryon, Phillip
Ramey, John
Rea, William; James, Senr.
Renno, Stephen
Roach, John
Rea, John
Rice, William
Redman, Rhoda
Roberts, James; William
Reynolds, Bartlett
Redman, Ignatious
Right, Samuel
Reynolds, Moses

Rice, Daniel; Spencer
Rogers, David; George
Richardson, Henry
Reynolds, Richard
Ratliff, Silas; John
Rentfro, William
Radford, John
Redd, John
Ramsey, John
Richmond, William
Rowland, Baldwin
Reeves, George
Read, William
Rowland, Michael
Reno, John
Rowland, John, Senr.
Rea, John
Reynolds, George; Richard
Rich, John; William
Renn, Benjamin
Roberson, Richard
Ross, David
Roberson, John; George; Thomas; Thomas, Jr.
Randolph, Samuel
Redman, James
Ryan, William
Richardson, Amos, Jr.; Amos, Senr.
Ray, David
Richardson, Daniel
Rower, Frederick, Capt.
Ringo, Cornelius
Richardson, Stanup
Rentfro, Joshua
Richards, Shadrick
Rutter, Abraham
Richards, Edward
Ramsey, John; George
Rubell, Owen
Roach, John
Ryan, Darby
Roberts, Thomas
Ross, Daniel
Reel, Michael
Rentfro, John
Roles, Christopher
Richards, Thomas

Shaw, Josiah
Stallings, Jacob
Spratley, James
Smith, Thomas
Sams, John; William, Senr.
Scroggins, George
Smith, John
Simmons, John
Swanson, William
Sandford, John
Sturgion, Ambrose
Shelton, Samuel
Sowell, William
Spencer, James, Senr.
Scott, Burrell
Shelton, James, Capt.
Solomon, Drury
Spencer, James, Jr.
Shelton, William
Smith, Bradley; Thomas
Sharp, William
Simmons, Zacheriah
Smith, Anthony; Josiah; William; Zadock
Stockton, Thomas
Sims, Sarah; Mathew; Bartlett
Stults, George
Shelton, Ralph, Senr.; Eliphaz
Smith, Henry
Shelton, Palatiah
Sims, John
Sowell, Joseph
Smith, Isaac
Street, Joseph
Small, John; Mathew
Stinnett, Benjamin
Smith, John
Salmon, Rowland
Sneed, John
Short, James
Smith, Daniel
Sims, Ignatious
Sumter, Henry
Searcey, Robert
Stamps, John
Salmon, John
Scruggs, Julius
Stockton, Robert
Stokes, John
Stennate, James
Stephens, John; William
Scales, Joseph
Smith, Robert
Stuart, Murdock, William
Smith, Edward
Stephens, William; Sampson
Scoggins, Humphry
Swanson, William, Jr.
Shrewsberry, Jeremiah
Standeford, Israel
Strange, James
Spaulden, Thomas
Swillivant, John
Stephens, John
Smith, John; John (Bull Run); Thomas, Capt.
Swanson, William, Senr.
Sherwood, Robert
Smith, Joseph; Peter
Shoemate, Daniel
Swanson, Nathan
Shockley, Levy
Stobes, Jacob
Stewart, James, Jr.; James, Senr.; William

Standefore, James
Sanders, Peter
Standefore, Luke
Smith, Daniel; Gidoney; John
Stanton, Richard
Spangler, Daniel; Daniel, Jr.
Stiout, Joseph
Stout, Samuel
Standefore, William
Stanley, John; Robert; William
Sherendon, Phillip
Stanley, William; Richard
Stanton, John
Stockton, Robert
Swann, Jonathan
Standford, George
Swillivant, Thomas
Saunders, William; John
Smith, Munford; Bartlett; Randall
Stewart, James; John; John, Senr.
Smith, Joseph
Solomon, Isham
Street, Samuel
Stephens, William; Dudley
Smith, William, Senr.; William, Jr.

Taylor, James
Tunning, Thomas
Thomas, Austin
Taylor, George; William
Thompson, James
Thomas, Charles
Tittle, Anthoney
Tenison, Zaphaniah
Tate, Nathaniel
Turner, Josiah
Tate, Henry; Robert
Thomas, Phillip
Turner, William; William; Sharick; John
Tarrant, Samuel
Tunstall, William
Tackett, William
Tarrant, James; Mary
Tankersley, John; Richard
Thomas, John
Thomason, Turner; William, Senr.; Richard; William, Jr.
Tillason, Francis
Tarrant, Leonard
Threlkeld, Thomas
Thompson, William
Thomson, Sherwood
Tate, Caleb
Troop, Jacob
Tharp, William

Veal, Nathan
Vinson, Ezekeal; William
Vernale, Richard

Walling, Elisha
Willingham, Jessee
Wilson, James
Webb, Thomas; Robert; Morriss
Williams, Joseph; Garrott
Witt, David
Webb, Elizabeth
Wilkinson, William
Watson, John
Wilson, William
Welch, Richard
Walker, Samuel
Witt, Jesse
Wolverton, Andrew
Webb, William
Weatherspoon, William
Wilson, Harris
Willis, Joseph, Thomas, Senr.; John
Warden, Robert
Williams, James
Walden, Aaron
Witt, John
Webster, Joseph
Watson, John
Warwock, Jacob
Waller, George
Webster, Reuben
Wilson, Daniel; James; Thomas; Moses; Martha
Warren, Henry
Ware, John
Williams, John
Watson, David
Williams, William; Elizabeth
Watson, Robert
Wheat, Benjamin
Wood, Elliott
Wells, John
Woodall, John
Willis, David; Esaiah
Woods, Robert; John; Hugh; George
Warren, William
Webb, Samuel
Woods, Joseph
Warren, Zackariah; Thomas (2); Drury
Webb, William; Smith; Henry Robert
Walker, Joel
Wade, Bartlett
Walton & Calloway
Wade, James
Webb, Isham; William
Wrial, John
Watson, Robert
Watkins, George
Williams, William; Thomas

Young, Ridley; Peter;

Young cont'd.
  William; James; John

May 2, 1780.
Received of the Commissioners of Henry County a copy of the foregoing List which I promised.
The same agreeable to Law.

                                George Hairston, Sh.
Teste:
Geo. Waller
John Salmon